# Allergies

# Allergies

## Elaine Landau

**TWENTY-FIRST CENTURY BOOKS**

A Division of Henry Holt and Company
New York

Twenty-First Century Books
A Division of Henry Holt and Company, Inc.
115 West 18th Street
New York, NY 10011

Henry Holt ® and colophon are trademarks of
Henry Holt and Company, Inc.
*Publishers since 1866*

**Library of Congress Cataloging-in-Publication Data**
Landau, Elaine.
Allergies / Elaine Landau. — 1st ed.
p. cm. — (Understanding illness)
Includes index.
1. Allergy—Juvenile literature. [1. Allergy.]
I. Title. II Series: Landau, Elaine. Understanding illness.
RC585.L34 1994
616.97—dc20                                   94-13831
                                                    CIP
                                                    AC
ISBN 0-8050-2989-3
First Edition 1994

Printed in the United States of America
All first editions are printed on acid-free paper ∞.
10  9  8  7  6  5  4  3  2  1

**Photo Credits**

p. 15: R. Feldman/Visuals Unlimited; p. 16: George White Location
Photography; p. 18: Ben Klaffke; p. 19: Visuals Unlimited/L. J. Connor; p. 21:
Visuals Unlimited: M. and D. Long; pp. 28 (both), 37: Visuals Unlimited; p. 31:
Billy E. Barnes/Transparencies, Inc.; p. 32: Dennis Barnes; p. 34: Visuals
Unlimited/Cabisco; p. 35: Visuals Unlimited/Linda H. Hopson; p. 40: NIAID,
NIH; pp. 42, 45, 47: National Jewish Center for Immunology and
Respiratory Medicine; p. 50: Deither Endlicher/Wide World Photos, Inc.

For Jeremiah Tudor

# CONTENTS

.

# Allergies

# CHAPTER
## ONE

# Something's Wrong

Twelve-year-old Daniel loved the outdoors and had enjoyed nature since he was young. His family always vacationed in national parks and spent most spring weekends backpacking along wooded trails. But one summer Daniel's relish for nature was lessened by a new problem: the boy began to feel miserable during the warm-weather outings he once liked so much. After being outdoors he'd have a stuffy nose, watery, itchy eyes, and sneezing and coughing fits.

That summer was especially disappointing for another young person as well. Ellen, a fifth grader, had to say good-bye to her best friend, Carly, because Carly's family was moving to the West Coast. The girls promised to faithfully write each other and as a token of their friendship, they exchanged inexpensive friendship rings.

Both vowed never to take the rings off, but before the week was over Ellen had to break her promise. At first her skin beneath the ring had just itched badly, but after a day or two it became red and irritated. The gift from Carly had meant a great deal to her. Ellen was sorry to learn that she was allergic to the nickel in the ring.

More than 1,000 miles (1,600 kilometers) away 11-year-old Ilana had a frightening experience at about the same time. She had been reading a book in her bedroom, when a wasp flew in through an open window and stung her. The girl quickly realized that she couldn't continue reading, as she began to feel hot and itchy all over. Finding it difficult to walk, she called downstairs to her mother for help. Her mother phoned the doctor, who told them not to waste any time getting to the emergency room of the local hospital. En route to the facility, Ilana vomited and felt even worse. By the time they reached the hospital, the young girl had stopped breathing. Fortunately, the hospital's medical staff revived her.

That fall a high-school junior named Jonathan and several of his friends took a weekend tour on horseback through the Rocky Mountains. Their guide led the way while the young men followed behind, enjoying the scenery and crisp pine-scented mountain air. However, after a few hours, Jonathan became ill. His chest felt tight and his breathing had a wheezy sound to it. At first Jonathan wasn't concerned, thinking that he was just adjusting to the high altitude. But, as the hours passed, his condition worsened. After telling the guide what was happening, the group stopped at a post along the way where Jonathan received medical help. As it turned out, the teenager had a severe allergy to horses.

While these cases differ somewhat, a common thread runs through them. In each instance someone either experienced a degree of discomfort or was severely endangered due to an allergic reaction. Although allergies are often treated lightly, these cases show that they can range from annoying to potentially lethal. Various allergies affect a broad range of people throughout the world. It's difficult to get exact statistics, since people frequently mistake allergies for colds or try to handle allergic reactions without seeing a doctor.

Yet the National Institute of Allergy and Infectious Diseases of the National Institutes of Health reports that between 40 million and 50 million Americans suffer from allergies. Each year more than $600 million is spent on allergy medications. In addition, 10 percent of all visits to a doctor are to seek allergy relief.[1]

This book is about allergies—how they occur and what can be done to relieve them.

# CHAPTER TWO

## *Allergies*

Most people know someone who is allergic to something. Allergies affect people of all races and ages throughout the world. But not everyone knows how and why allergies occur.

People become allergic to a substance when their bodies mistakenly act to protect them from what it believes is a hazardous condition. As Dr. Charles H. Banov, associate professor of medicine and bacteriology-immunology at the Medical University of South Carolina and past president of the American College of Allergists, explained the process, "The immune system normally protects the body against harmful invaders, but in allergic people, it reacts to innocuous [harmless] substances like dust and pollen."[1]

Our bodies produce antibodies (proteins in the blood) to fight infection and disease. Scientists think that people who develop allergies may produce more than the normal amount of an antibody, or immunoglobulin, known as IgE. The IgE antibodies attach themselves to cells called mast cells, which line the outer surface of the nose, throat, and lungs. In the presence of allergy-producing substances, such as dust or pollen, the IgE antibodies stimulate the mast cells to manufacture biochemicals

*Immunoglobin (above) plays an
important role in allergies.*

such as histamine. Histamine and similar acting chemical substances cause the sneezing, itchy, watery eyes, and other symptoms that characterize many allergies.

There are a large number of allergens (allergy-producing substances) in the environment. Among those most often discussed is the pollen from plants (including grasses and trees) that causes hay fever. Hay fever has nothing to do with hay or fever. Instead, it is a condition resulting from the tons of microscopic pollen released during the warmer months. Although the pollen drifts through the air to eventually fertilize other plants, often it doesn't reach its target. Instead it enters people's noses and throats, triggering seasonal allergies. Hay fever as well as similar allergies are medically known as sea-

*Mildew, a fungus growth, is a common allergen.*

sonal allergic rhinitis. "Rhinitis" means an inflammation of the nose's mucous membranes (the soft, smooth, moist tissue lining the cavities of the nose).

Allergies that persist throughout the year are known as perennial allergic rhinitis. Two common allergens in this category are mold and dust. Mold can be found all around us. Indoor molds often come from basements, bathrooms, air conditioners, and humidifiers. Outside, decaying leaves and grass release mold spores. Dust is another widespread allergen. It contains microscopic creatures known as dust mites that live on tiny particles of hair and dead skin. Dust mites, as well as their dead bodies and stools, are allergens as well.

Many people are also allergic to animals. At one

time it was thought that allergies to pets were due to animal dander—the microscopic flakes of skin that come off of animals having fur or feathers. However, researchers have since learned that the true allergen is probably also the proteins in the saliva present on the dander. Cats are responsible for the most severe of these allergic reactions. That's largely because they preen themselves more than other furry pets. The preening contaminates the environment with cat allergens that can be in very small particles that fly about easily. These allergens become airborne and are breathed in by humans.

Some people experience allergic skin reactions. Atopic dermatitis and contact dermatitis are conditions that result in rashes, blisters, or scaly patches. Atopic dermatitis, which affects about 1 percent of the population, starts with itching and progresses to a rash. While the process is still not clearly understood, the antibody IgE is also thought to be at fault here. Contact dermatitis, a more common skin irritation, is frequently sparked by poison ivy, poison oak, and poison sumac, as well as by various chemicals and metals such as nickel. Jewelry items made from inexpensive metals containing nickel often provoke this reaction when such a necklace, bracelet, ring, or earrings touch the skin. It can also be triggered in certain individuals by some drugs, perfumes, fabrics, and cosmetics. Contact dermatitis results when the body's white blood cells incorrectly fight a substance it perceives as a danger.

Among the most serious allergic reactions are those that result in anaphylactic shock. Anaphylactic shock, or anaphylaxis, is the medical term used to describe the frightening and sometimes deadly allergic reaction some

*Poison oak may look harmless, but it can cause considerable discomfort.*

people experience after being stung by a wasp or other insect, eating certain foods, taking a particular medication, or even engaging in vigorous exercise. Although these reactions are uncommon, they can nevertheless occur in individuals who've developed an extreme sensitivity to a certain substance.

It's important for people prone to anaphylaxis to be aware of its initial symptoms. The person may suddenly feel itchy and hot, and in some cases there may be hives, swelling, nausea, a pounding heart, difficulty breathing, and a drop in blood pressure.

It's estimated that about 50 to 100 people die every year as the result of insect stings. The true number may actually be higher. Doctors suspect that some people found dead outdoors and believed to be heart attack vic-

*Here a beekeeper wears protective
garb to avoid being stung.*

tims may actually have died from insect stings. Most
sting reactions that result in death occur among people
who've never been stung before. A study conducted at
Johns Hopkins University revealed that about 10 percent
of the population may be at risk for such extreme reactions. People who've been stung often (such as beekeep-
ers) are at higher risk than the average person. So is
anyone who had previously experienced a reaction from
a sting.

Allergic food reactions can result in hives, wheezing, itching, and even anaphylaxis. But many people who believe they are allergic to foods really aren't. According to the National Jewish Center for Immunology and Respiratory Medicine, while about 40 percent of adults claim to be allergic to certain foods, the true figure is closer to between 0.1 and 5 percent.[2] Although many children have food allergies, they usually outgrow them by the time they are three. Unfortunately, large numbers of individuals continue to avoid these foods into adulthood despite the fact that they may not have been allergic to them since they were toddlers.

Other factors can lead people to mistakenly believe they're allergic to particular foods as well. In some cases it may simply be a matter of coincidence. Someone unknowingly experiencing a mild stomach flu or other virus might easily blame the symptoms on something he or she ate. At other times, reactions to spoiled or contaminated foods have been mistaken for allergies. Not knowing the facts has also led some people to mistakenly think of some foods, such as chocolate and strawberries, as common allergens. However, very few people are actually allergic to either.

The foods people are genuinely allergic to include eggs, milk, shellfish, fish, and peanuts. Unfortunately, even a small amount of these foods can be troublesome to someone allergic to them. Food preservatives known as sulfites have been identified as culprits as well. As a result, these preservatives have been banned from use in salad bars and restaurants.

Drug allergies are equally serious. It's estimated that between 3 and 5 percent of the population is allergic to

*Shrimp are among the foods known to*
*cause severe allergic reactions in some people.*

penicillin. Sulfa drugs as well as insulin, aspirin, and injectable dyes used for X rays and other medical tests have been known to trigger similar reactions in some individuals. Still another medication associated with allergic reactions is chymopapain. Chymopapain, which comes from the papaya tree, is frequently used in treating severe back injuries. At times avoiding chymopapain can be tricky since it is also used in some meat tenderizers, pills to aid digestion, toothpastes, and cleaning fluids for soft contact lenses.

An unusual type of physical allergy known as exercise-induced (brought on by exercise) anaphylaxis has proven extremely troublesome to a small group of individuals. It can occur in either warm or cool weather and usually begins with an itch that soon progresses to hives, choking, fainting, or even more serious symptoms. People who fall victim to exercise-induced anaphylaxis may suffer from other allergies as well. According to Dr. Albert L. Sheffer, clinical professor of medicine at Harvard Medical School, "No one is sure what causes exercise-induced anaphylaxis, but about half of the patients who get it also have asthma, hay fever, or eczema, and two thirds have family histories of allergies. . . . There's increasing evidence that some people who may be sensitive to certain foods [shellfish, celery, some fruits] manifest their allergy only if they exercise after ingesting these foods."[3]

Why are some people affected by allergies and others not? According to James Wells, allergy specialist and professor of medicine at the University of Oklahoma Health Sciences Center, the tendency toward allergies runs in families. He noted, "We don't yet know all the nuts and bolts of just how they are inherited. Overall, the odds of developing allergies are about 15 percent, but that goes up to 35 percent if one parent is allergic, and to nearly 50 percent if both parents are allergic. However, children are typically not allergic to the same things as their parents."[4]

Recent research has also uncovered a connection between allergy and personality. Iris R. Bell, M.D. Ph.D., an assistant professor of psychiatry at the University of Arizona College of Medicine in Tucson, questioned 375 college students as to their temperaments and whether or not they had ever had allergies.

The results were intriguing. Bell found that the introverted, or less-outgoing, students were the most likely to suffer from hay fever. Six out of 18 students who rated themselves as quite shy had the allergy, while none of the 19 very outgoing students in the study had allergies. The researchers think shyness may be genetically linked to hay fever the way other inherited traits, such as red hair and freckles, are connected.

There's additional evidence to support the tie between shyness and hay fever. A study by Dr. Jerome Kagan of Harvard University found shyness to be an identifiable temperament trait among children with allergies. Kagan further cited other data that indicate a greater incidence of hay fever among close relatives of very shy children.

Yet other scientists dispute these conclusions. They feel that any link between shyness and hay fever has more to do with environment or lifestyle than heredity. As Dr. Jonathan Cheek, professor of psychology at Wellesley College in Massachusetts put it, "Extremely shy people lead stressful lives. They suffer physiological symptoms such as a pounding heart, upset stomach, and dry mouth. . . . That kind of psychosocial stress is believed to lower immune functioning."[5] Since allergies occur when the immune system mistakenly fights a substance that isn't normally harmful, could the individual's stress level be more relevant than his or her genetic makeup?

Still other studies have been conducted on the emotional aspects of allergies. Some of the work was prompted by the fact that at times allergic reactions occur without the allergen that usually triggers them. Scientists wanted to learn if an individual's emotional state or feelings alone were sufficient to cause an allergic reaction.

To explore this possibility a group of psychologists and immunologists at McMaster University in Ontario, Canada, had laboratory rats develop an allergy to egg whites. The rats were divided into two groups. One group received egg white shots while being exposed to flashing lights and humming sounds for 15 minutes. The other group had their egg white shots 24 hours after hearing and seeing the stimuli. Due to the length of time between the shots and the commotion, the second rat group did not connect one with the other—but the first group did.

When the rats were later exposed to the humming sounds and flashing lights without the shots, the rats that originally experienced them at the same time had an allergic reaction. Apparently the lights and hums now had the same effect on their immune systems as the allergen (egg whites) had. These results suggest that the immune system can be made to respond to something seen, heard, or felt, as it would to a recognized allergy trigger.

The researchers concluded that if an animal can be conditioned to have an allergic reaction to a sight or sound, the brain must be involved. However, it still isn't clear whether or not the human mind could actually trigger or perhaps even prevent an allergic reaction. Dr. Dean Metcalfe, an immunologist at the National Institute of Allergy and Infectious Diseases, expressed his doubts about findings connecting allergies with human behavior when he said, "As a scientist you can't dismiss the evidence: it does suggest that the nervous system can do something that affects the cells that are the main triggers of an allergic response. But is it possible to ring a bell and cause an allergic reaction in humans? As a clinician I don't see the evidence. Until I do I'm going to relegate this effect to a minor role."[6]

It's generally agreed that additional research is needed to determine what such findings mean for humans. Yet the possibilities are exciting. Knowing more about allergies could lead to a broader understanding of this widespread problem as well as to improved treatment methods.

# CHAPTER
## THREE

# Diagnosis and Treatment

Fifteen-year-old Mike thought he had a winter cold that had dragged on for months. Some days he felt he was getting better. But then his stuffy nose and itchy, watery eyes would return, causing him to feel even worse than before.

At first Mike, who was extremely active in both school and sports, thought up different reasons for the way he felt. When his parents noticed that he wasn't getting over his cold, he insisted that being around as many kids as he was continually exposed him to germs. He'd always promise to get more rest, remember to take his vitamins, and take better care of himself. However, after nothing seemed to help, Mike's parents made him see a doctor. It was only then that he and his family realized that what they had mistaken for a cold was actually an allergy to dust and mold.

Diagnosing allergies is generally not a simple procedure. Therefore people with allergies may want to see an allergist—a doctor who specializes in diagnosing and treating these conditions. The physician must gather the patient's complete medical history including such information as when and where the symptoms appeared, how the patient spends his or her time (major activities and hobbies), whether the patient has any pets, and other background data. The person's answers to these and similarly revealing questions allow the physician to zero in on the allergies that may be causing the problem. The doctor will also probably perform standard skin tests on the patient, as this is a simple and reliable means of evaluating the patient's reaction to different allergens. Skin tests tend to be inexpensive and only cause the patient minimal discomfort.

There are various types of skin tests for allergies. In these procedures a diluted sample of an allergen is injected under the patient's skin or is applied to a scratch or puncture made on the back or arm. Different allergens can be tested on various portions of a person's back during the same office visit so the patient can find out how he or she reacts to more than one substance. If there's an allergic response, a small raised reddened area will appear at the test site. While the size of the red area will be significant to the doctor in the diagnosis, it is not positive proof that the person's symptoms are caused by that particular allergen.

According to Dr. Michael Kaliner, chief of the allergic-disease section of the National Institute of Allergy and Infectious Diseases, a branch of the National Institutes of Health in Bethesda, Maryland, "A detailed medical history is more important than any tests. If you screened the entire population with skin tests, 25 to 50 percent would have positive results. But that just means they have antibodies against the material you are testing. It doesn't mean they are symptomatic [show any allergic symptoms]. An active allergy is diagnosed by medical history, which is then confirmed by skin testing."[1]

At times allergists have their patients take blood

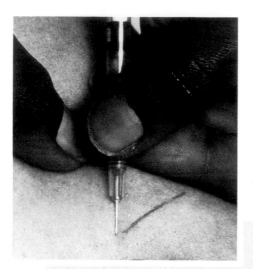

*This shows reactions following injections of sample allergens.*

tests to detect allergies. This may be done in place of or in addition to the skin tests. The various blood tests used for this purpose are called RAST (radioallergosorbent test), FAST (fluoro-allergosorbent test), and MAST (multiple antigen simultaneous testing). A single blood sample can be used to test for numerous allergies.

Blood tests are especially helpful in situations where a patient has a skin condition that makes skin testing difficult. A doctor may also use blood tests if he or she thinks a patient is so sensitive to an allergen that a skin test could be harmful. However, some physicians feel that allergy blood tests tend not to be as sensitive as skin testing, and these procedures are also more costly.

In allergy testing it's important that patients avoid questionable techniques that are not scientifically valid. One of these processes that the American Academy of Allergy and Immunology considers unproven and of no diagnostic value is cytotoxic testing. Here a possible allergen is added to a blood sample to see if there's a reaction.

It's also essential to be wary of false claims and quackery within the field. At one time a licensed doctor in Costa Mesa, California, ran a newspaper ad claiming that his testing lab could speedily identify various food allergies. A patient only had to send in a blood sample along with $300 to learn which foods should be avoided. In investigating the doctor's claims, the U.S. Food and Drug Administration (FDA) sent a sample of cow's blood to the lab under the pretense of it being a human's. The incorrect diagnosis returned had a humorous twist to it: the lab claimed that the cow was allergic to milk!

After identifying the troublesome allergens in medically ethical situations, the doctor will devise a treatment plan for the individual. Whenever possible, patients are urged to avoid what they are allergic to. However, this is easier to do if someone is allergic to penicillin or a particular brand of cosmetics than if dust or pollen is the problem.

Nevertheless some of the following allergy survival tips may prove helpful. Many of these suggestions can be done by a young person—others require assistance from an adult.

Avoid smoke. Smoking has been known to aggravate hay fever and other allergies. Stay away from smoky rooms and friends and family members while they're smoking.

Avoid pollen. If possible, don't plan outdoor activities in the morning during allergy season. That's when pollen levels are highest. Sunny, windy days are the worst.

People with pollen allergies who must work outdoors can purchase face masks designed to filter pollen out of the air. Face masks are available at many drugstores.

Lawns should be mowed so the grass is short (so they don't pollinate), and leaves raked and bagged. But this should never be done by the allergic person. It's preferable for that individual to do other chores instead.

Individuals with dust allergies should try to dust-proof their bedrooms. Keep all clothing in closed closets. Wool items should be placed in plastic bags. If there's an opportunity to redecorate, choose shades instead of venetian blinds, since blinds are notorious dust collectors. If curtains are used, pick a fabric that can be periodically washed in hot water to kill dust mites. Ideally, the bed mattress should be encased in a zippered plastic dust-proof cover. Only washable blankets, pillows, and mattress pads should be used, and these items should be frequently laundered. While all carpeting traps dust, shag

*A young person wears a protective
mask while working in a greenhouse
to guard against allergies.*

carpets are the worst. Tile, hardwood, or linoleum floors
are preferable. For added warmth, washable throw rugs
can be purchased.

If possible avoid cluttered rooms with overstuffed
furniture and shelves filled with knickknacks. Minimal
decoration is easier on allergy sufferers.

*Keeping a clean, dust-free house*
*can help reduce allergy symptoms.*

Water is an excellent dust remover. Washable items should be cleaned often in hot water. Dusting with a damp cloth or oiled rags should be done routinely.

As some allergic symptoms can be triggered by common household cleaners, the following choices are good alternatives:

- Baking soda—use for general cleaning and deodorizing.
- Beeswax, raw linseed oil, mineral oil, olive oil, paste wax—use to polish furniture.
- Nonchlorine bleach—use as household or laundry cleaner.
- Club soda—useful spot remover.
- Salt—works as a kitchen cleanser; loosens burned-on foods.

Trade vacuuming for a chore that won't aggravate your allergies. To avoid unnecessary dust inhalation, leave the room when someone else is vacuuming.

Ideally a home should be well-ventilated. This includes properly maintaining the heating and air-conditioning systems when possible.

Avoid pets with fur or feathers. Cats are usually worse than dogs and should not be in the home of someone with allergies. But dogs can still be a problem. Driving with an animal in the car can also be a source of heavy exposure because of the small space. Cockroaches are a major cause of year-round allergies as well.

Avoid places and objects in which mold flourishes. This means:

*A mildew-covered shoe, like the one shown here, could be a problem for an allergic person.*

- not having live plants, dried plants, or flowers in your room,
- spending as little time as possible in damp basements, musty bathrooms, or shower stalls,
- not cleaning out the garbage pails or bread boxes.

When buying clothes remember that many fabrics (such as permanent-press garments) are treated with the chemical formaldehyde to keep them wrinkle-free. But before washing, the combination of warm weather and high humidity or sweat can release the formaldehyde from the

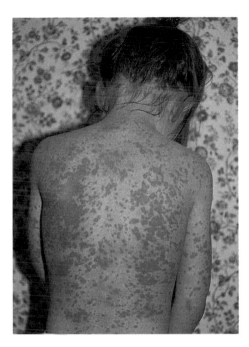

*An allergic skin
reaction can result in
a painful irritating
rash requiring
medical treatment.*

cloth on to the body. As a result the wearer may develop
an itchy rash. Formaldehyde-free fabrics include the nat-
ural fibers, such as silk, linen, and cotton.

Clothes should not be dried outdoors. Although they
acquire a fresh scent, the garments pick up airborne
pollen and molds.

In situations where it's especially difficult to avoid
or control troublesome allergens, medication may be necessary. For some people over-the-counter drugs work
well. However, these medications may cause drowsiness.
If used regularly over a prolonged period they may also
lose their effectiveness as the person's body becomes
used to, or develops a tolerance for, them.

Antihistamines (drugs to control allergic symptoms) that do not cause drowsiness are available through a doctor. Some of these medications come in pill form, while others are nasal sprays. At times patients must take these drugs routinely throughout the allergy season—often the sprays must be used for several days before maximum relief is achieved.

People who suffer from skin allergies may be given corticoid creams or ointments by their doctors. As these are powerful drugs, it's crucial to carefully follow the application directions and not use them for a longer time or in larger amounts than indicated. Besides avoiding the allergen(s) responsible for the condition, the person should try not to further irritate the affected skin area. That means limiting contact with soap and harsh chemicals.

Individuals whose allergic reactions result in life-threatening anaphylaxis must receive immediate medical attention. Usually they are injected with the drug epinephrine, also called Adrenalin, which rapidly acts to relieve symptoms. Sometimes oxygen and other medications may also be necessary to assist the victim in breathing.

If the allergen that caused the anaphylaxis is particularly hard to avoid, additional precautions should be taken. Some physicians have these people carry an epinephrine syringe designed for self use. Such syringes are only available by prescription and the patient must be thoroughly trained in their use. If the medication were accidently injected into a vein, serious health consequences could result.

*A medical alert bracelet (shown above)*
*lists illnesses, including what the wearer is*
*allergic to, and can be essential in an emergency.*

Allergy sufferers may try immunotherapy, or allergy shots, when avoiding allergens and taking pills and nasal sprays are not effective. In immunotherapy, patients receive injections of increasing amounts of the allergens that have been troublesome to them. These injections act to desensitize the body, reducing the level of IgE antibodies in the blood. They also serve to produce a protective antibody called IgG. Treatment continues until the patient's symptoms are considerably lessened. About 85 percent of immunotherapy patients who suffer from hay fever experience a reduction in both their symptoms and their need for medication within 24 months.[2]

Although all allergies cannot be prevented or completely controlled, in many cases the measures described here can go a long way toward making the patient's life more pleasant.

# CHAPTER FOUR

# Asthma

It was a beautiful Saturday morning and everyone in Jamie Cisco's (name changed) house busily prepared for the day ahead. That is everyone except Jamie. Although no one noticed her there at first, the ten-year-old girl sat slumped in a living room chair trying to catch her breath. She felt a tightness in her chest that made her think she was about to suffocate. Fortunately, moments later, Jamie's older sister found her. By then Jamie was gasping, wheezing, and unable to lift herself from the chair.

Although Jamie couldn't speak, she didn't need to. Her sister only had to see her struggling to breathe to know that the small girl needed help immediately. Within minutes their mother rushed Jamie to the hospital emergency room. The ten-year-old had asthma and was having a bad attack.

Asthma is a chronic (ongoing) lung disease that can severely limit the person's ability to breathe. The asthmatic's airways become inflamed and increasingly sensitive to various allergens that can result in asthmatic symptoms. During an asthma attack, the inside lining of the bronchi (the tubes that carry air into and out of the lungs) swell and constrict while the bronchial muscles

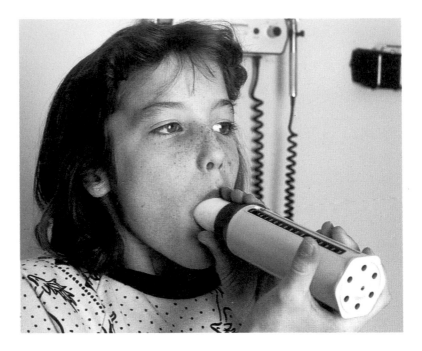

*A young person taking a pulmonary (lung) function test.*

around the tubes go into spasm. Mucus also collects in the tubes, further impairing the person's breathing ability. Many asthmatics claim that during attacks they feel as if they are breathing through a thin straw.

The most common symptoms of asthma include wheezing, coughing, shortness of breath, tightening of the chest, and mucus production. Frequently a persistent cough or cold signals the first stage of the disease. Some young asthmatics never develop wheezing, perhaps asthma's best known symptom. Dr. Robert F. Lemanske, Jr., a pediatric allergist at the University of Wisconsin, noted that it's often especially difficult to diagnose asthma in very young children since it's hard for them to follow the necessary directions for lung function tests.[1]

Asthma attacks frequently occur in response to various "triggers" in the patient's environment. Dr. Hyman Chai, senior staff physician of pediatrics and medicine at the National Jewish Center for Immunology and Respiratory Medicine, cites allergies as the most widely known cause of the allergic inflammation that causes asthma. Between 50 and 80 percent of the people who have asthma also have severe allergies.[2] In the majority of cases, they've suffered from both allergies and asthma since childhood. A heavy pollen season, eating a single shrimp, or playing with a neighbor's dog may be sufficient to bring on an asthma attack in some of these individuals.

Asthma attacks can also be triggered by irritants such as air pollution and various chemicals, tobacco smoke, certain foods, viral infections, and breathing in cold air. Still other asthma triggers include exercise, laughing hard, sinusitis (inflammation of the lining of the sinuses), emotions, sensitivity to aspirin and food additives, and strong odors. Depending on the individual and the circumstances, asthma symptoms can range from mild to severe. Some asthmatics generally only experience symptoms during a particular season, while others deal with possible attacks throughout the year.

Statistics on asthma from the Centers for Disease Control in Atlanta, Georgia, are not encouraging. Its incidence has risen in recent years and many of these cases are more severe than in the past. Approximately 10 mil-

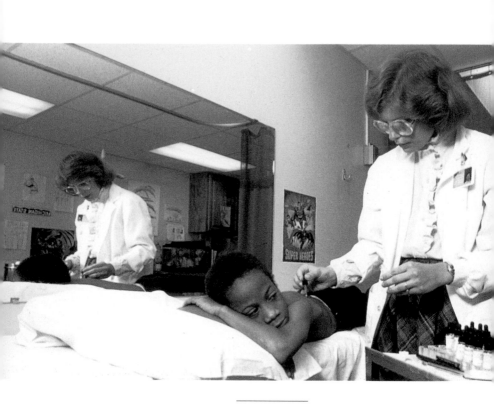

*Childhood asthma has steadily increased and is the leading cause of hospitalization among young people.*

lion Americans had asthma in 1993 as compared with 6.8 million in 1980. Two and a half million of these are children. Hospital admissions for asthma have tripled from 1978 to 1987 and asthma death rates rose 68 percent from 1980 to 1989 as well.[3]

Scientists are not sure of the reason for this increase. As Dr. Gail Shapiro, clinical professor of pediatrics at the University of Washington School of Medicine in Seattle, Washington, stated, "A decrease in access to good medical care, overuse of medications for symptomatic relief, and increased pollution and allergies have all been suggested as contributing factors. But no definite proof exists for any one cause."[4] The problem isn't limited to the United States. Increased numbers of children dying from asthma have also been reported in Australia, Great Britain, and New Zealand.

Although anyone can get asthma, the illness tends to strike certain groups more than others. Children develop asthma more often than adults, but asthma can develop at any age. The illness is the leading cause of admission to children's hospitals. Asthma is also the most common cause of school absenteeism. In all developed countries boys develop asthma early in childhood about twice as often as girls, but girls at least partially catch up in their teens. African-Americans are more likely than whites to become asthmatic and are nearly twice as likely to die from the illness.

However, these death rate differences are due to class and economic differences rather than race. As Dr. Herbert C. Mansmann, Jr., associate professor of pediatrics at Thomas Jefferson University Medical Center in Philadelphia, said, "To me, it's a socioeconomic problem. [African-Americans] come in too late, too severely ill and too sick for too long. Some get . . . [only emergency] care, then go home and don't have enough money to buy the medicine they need so they're back in the emergency room a week later. The disease just smolders along like a fire and it never goes out."[5]

It's not known why some people (even within the same family) develop asthma and others don't. Even though the disease can't be cured, with proper treatment it can usually be effectively controlled. Early diagnosis is an important factor in treating asthma. But sometimes diagnosing milder cases can be tricky since they mimic a number of other medical conditions. Therefore it's important for the physician to secure the patient's complete medical history as well as carefully evaluate the symptoms. The person's response to asthma medications should also be noted.

Ideally a patient's medical examination will include breathing tests, which are done either in the doctor's office or hospital, to reveal any blockage of the air passages. The doctor may also want chest and sinus X rays, a complete blood work, checks of the mucus secretions in the lungs and nose, and an evaluation of the patient's response to exercise. In addition, most asthmatics are tested for allergies, as allergens frequently trigger asthma attacks.

Since asthma is a chronic condition, sufferers should be monitored by a doctor periodically. The physician will note the condition of the patient's lungs as well as any asthmatic symptoms. Frequently, prior to a full-blown asthma attack, the person will experience some early warning signs. These include sneezing, headaches, mood swings, differences in breathing, a stuffed or runny nose, coughing, exhaustion, sleeping difficulties, an itchy throat or chin, and dark circles beneath the eyes.

Many people also monitor their asthma through an easy-to-use instrument known as a peak flow meter. The peak flow meter shows people how well their lungs are functioning by measuring the flow rate of exhaled air. A

*A young child being entertained*
*while taking a breathing test.*

drop in flow can serve as still another warning of an oncoming attack.

People with asthma must learn to effectively manage their illness. Whenever possible, recommended environmental changes should be made before resorting to continued medication. If the asthma is triggered by allergies, individuals should try to lessen their exposure to these allergens. Other substances that are not allergens but irritate an asthmatic's sensitive air passages should be avoided as well. Since cigarette smoke is among the most common of these, no one in the person's home should smoke. In many cases it's also a good idea for someone with asthma to stay away from aerosol sprays, perfumes, and heavy duty cleaning products, since strong odors can sometimes trigger an attack as well.

In the past, asthmatics frequently moved to other parts of the country hoping to find an environment in which their attacks were less likely to occur. However most doctors today believe there isn't any ideal location for someone with this illness. Although the person may seem to have improved one season, this could change the next. In some cases, whatever previously triggered the asthma attacks will also be present at the new residence. Other times the person has merely traded one set of asthma triggers for another.

When it's impossible to control a patient's asthma by eliminating what triggers the attacks, medication may be used. Depending upon the circumstances, a person may only take medication when needed or regularly to prevent or lessen breathing problems. Using medication routinely reduces the airway's inflammation and provides

*A young boy uses an inhaler to breathe in his
asthma medication for immediate relief.*

ongoing protection against symptoms. Some people with
asthma inhale their medication, since breathing in the
drug brings it directly to the airways. Others take their
drugs in pill form. Regardless of the treatment used,
someone with asthma should seek immediate medical
attention if he or she finds that the medication isn't working as it should.

In addition to the more traditional ways of treating
asthma, research has been conducted at the Minneapolis
Children's Medical Center on employing Relaxation
Mental Imagery (RMI) exercises to control the illness.
Young people using these self-hypnosis techniques were

told to focus on a particular idea or image to ward off asthma symptoms.

In evaluating 40 of these participants for up to two years afterward, 50 percent indicated that their asthma had improved as a result of practicing the techniques they'd learned. This was confirmed through a dramatic decrease in emergency room visits as well as less severe attacks and a reduced need for medication.

Among the study participants was $11\frac{1}{2}$-year-old Sherry (not real name) who was referred to the medical center by her family doctor. Although Sherry had asthma since she was young, the condition worsened as she grew older. Sherry's attacks frequently occurred in the middle of the night, causing her to lose sleep and have difficulty concentrating in school the next day. She was also unhappy over having to frequently leave class due to severe coughing fits.

After entering the program, Sherry learned a simple exercise she could use both at home and school when she was about to have an asthma attack. The young girl would simply imagine she'd been swimming at a beautiful beach and was now breathing comfortably on the shore.

Just a month following her last practice session, Sherry experienced a significant improvement. She no longer woke up gasping for breath at night or had to leave class because of her asthma. Before long, Sherry was able to discontinue her medication and rely on RMI techniques to control the few wheezing episodes she still experienced.

However, even after arriving at the most effective

treatment regime, some individuals with asthma still find it difficult to adjust to their illness. This may be especially true for young people. After extensively studying children with chronic illnesses, Dr. Lee Salk, professor of psychology, psychiatry, and pediatrics at the New York Hospital–Cornell Medical Center in New York City, found that many asthmatic young people feared dying as a result of not being able to breathe during an asthma attack. At various times, having asthma also made them feel angry, depressed, and inferior. Some of the youths studied thought being asthmatic made them a burden to their families.

Undeniably, asthma or any other serious illness can present problems. This may be especially so when asthma attacks are triggered by exercise. Exercise-induced asthma (EIA) tends to strike after five to ten minutes of stopping vigorous exertion. Many of these attacks are sparked by running and the problem may be aggravated if there's a high pollen level. At times young people have been kept by their parents from taking part in organized sports or even playing vigorously with their friends after school.

However, in recent years the situation has improved. Once the problem is identified these incidents can often be avoided by taking medication about 15 to 20 minutes before a scheduled activity to keep the bronchial passages open. Today most young people with asthma can take part in school sports and other physical activities.

The strides achieved by some asthmatic athletes are impressive. Champion bicyclist Alexei Grewal, Olympic cross-country skier Bill Koch, and Olympic javelin

*Learning to control her asthma helped
Jackie Joyner-Kersee win still another gold medal
during the 1992 Olympics in Barcelona, Spain.*

thrower Karin Smith have all won distinguished athletic awards despite having asthma. Olympic runner Jackie Joyner-Kersee refused to let asthma stop her from reaching new heights. In the 1988 Olympic Summer Games in Seoul, Korea, she won two gold medals and broke a world record.

However, the track-and-field star initially denied that asthma could ever diminish her performance and failed to take her medication regularly. The situation became a crisis while she was training just seven months before the Seoul Olympics. As Joyner-Kersee recalled, "It was an easy training day. We were running up the stadium steps and when I came off the last step I knew that something was really wrong with me. I couldn't breathe, but when I couldn't I started to panic. I tried taking off my clothes in an effort to get in more air. I used my inhaler, but after a few puffs, I still didn't get any better. I really felt as if I was getting ready to die."[6]

Jackie Joyner-Kersee was rushed to a hospital where she received emergency-room treatment for her severe asthma attack. The incident had been triggered by the combined effect of not taking her medication and exercising on a cold day while the stadium grass was being mowed. Her frightening experience made the celebrity athlete change her ways. After that she kept a small note tacked to her refrigerator door that reads: "Jackie, take your medication." She now knows that is something she doesn't want to forget.

Many experts feel the key for an asthmatic to achieve his or her full athletic potential lies in selecting the correct time, place, and medication before beginning an activity. This may mean avoiding outdoor exercise when it's extremely cold and windy or when the pollen count is very high. It's also wise to skip a workout if there are signs that the person's asthma is worsening. "You shouldn't force yourself to exercise when you're wheezing or tight," a physician who treats numerous asthmatics warned. "If you're already in trouble before you start exercising, you can place yourself in real jeopardy if you go through with it."[7]

Although some individuals outgrow their asthma, this isn't so for everyone. Therefore, it's important for people with asthma to find a workable balance. Studies performed at New York University Medical Center involving asthmatics showed that these individuals can often greatly benefit from a moderate degree of exercise. Being in good physical condition helps reduce asthma symptoms.

The advantages of exercise frequently become painfully obvious once people stop their workouts. That's what happened to Nancy Hogshead, an Olympic swimmer who won a silver and three gold medals for the United States in 1984. After the young woman stopped competing, her asthma became markedly worse. "The more out of shape I am, the more problems I have," she stated. "I cough, I have bronchitis, I get sick."[8]

Working with a specialist at the Allergy Center in Silver Spring, Maryland, Hogshead developed a beneficial exercise program for herself. She found that through exercise and medication she was able to enhance her athletic potential. Hogshead even created an instructional video called "Nancy Hogshead's Aerobics for Asthmatics."

Even active young people with asthma may still sometimes feel as if they are on an emotional roller-coaster. Asthma-related problems at school can often be troublesome. A national survey of school nurses revealed that 54 percent of public schools do not allow asthmatic students to carry their inhalers (a small device enabling the person to breathe in the medication) with them. Frequently inhalers must be left with the school nurse, as administrators fear other students might use the devices and be harmed. As a result, many young people with asthma must deal with not having ready access to their medication when symptoms occur.

Yet many young people throughout the country have learned to effectively cope. Part of their success lies in knowing as much as possible about asthma and taking an active role in their treatment program. A young person with asthma should learn what triggers the attacks as well as how to administer the medication. Understanding precisely what's happening and what can be done to relieve it will help the person work through an attack.

At times there may be teasing or questions from friends or classmates. Some young people with asthma find it useful to explain that needing a nebulizer (a shoe-box-size air compressor that turns liquid medication into a fine inhalable mist) or an inhaler to help them breathe is no different from the person who wears glasses to help him or her to see.

Young people with asthma should remember that their illness need not hold them back. In addition to numerous Olympic athletes, such famous celebrities as Elizabeth Taylor and Liza Minnelli have achieved international success despite being asthmatic.

Young asthma sufferers can learn more about their

illness at one of the growing number of summer camps sponsored by the American Lung Association. Many have also benefited from counseling and from self-help groups for young people with asthma. These support groups assure members that they are not alone—others have experienced what they've been through and are there to help. Knowing that won't cure their asthma, but may make it easier to handle.

# Epilogue

Twelve year-old Krista speaks: "I hated having allergies. My friends loved the warm weather and playing volleyball on the beach. But I hid out in air-conditioned rooms most of the time just so I could breathe. When there was pollen in the air my eyes got red and watery. I'd walk down the street carrying a wad of tissues and people would ask me why I was crying. They must have thought I was the saddest person in the world. It was humiliating."

Fortunately Krista found help for her problem. Her family doctor referred her to an allergist who came up with an effective medication regime for the young girl. The future also appears promising for Krista and the many other young people who suffer from allergies and/or asthma. Research to improve available testing and treatment methods is underway. Scientists are extensively studying the immune system's response to allergens and substances that trigger these reactions. Today their efforts are improving how these conditions can be controlled. One day allergies and asthma may be preventable as well.

# E N D
## NOTES

### CHAPTER 1
1. Steven Findlay, "Allergy Warfare," *U.S. News & World Report,* February 20, 1989, 69.

### CHAPTER 2
1. Gale Malesky, ed., "Best Bet Relief from Allergy Season from the American College of Allergists," *Prevention,* May 1987, 50.

2. National Jewish Center for Immunology and Respiratory Medicine, *Understanding Allergy* (Denver: National Jewish Center for Immunology and Respiratory Medicine, 1993), 6.

3. "Exercise Dangers," *Vogue,* November 1986, 180.

4. "What to Do When Food Bites Back," *USA Today,* October 1991, 3.

5. Linda Emanuel, "Sneezy Personalities," *Health,* February 1991, 17

6. "Pavlov's Rats," *Discover,* May 1989, 14.

### CHAPTER 3
1. Gale Malesky, ed., "Best Bet Relief from Allergy Season from the American College of Allergists," *Prevention,* May 1987, 53.

2. National Institute of Allergy and Infectious Diseases, *Something in the Air: Airborne Allergies* (Bethesda, Md.: Department of Health and Human Services, 1993), 26.

## CHAPTER 4

1. Barbara Kantrowitz, "The Breath of Life," *Newsweek,* Special Issue, Summer 1991, 52.

2. Carolyn Gloeckher, "Life with Asthma," *Current Health,* April 1989, 10.

3. Lucy Moll, "A Breath of Fresh Air," *Vegetarian Times,* July 1992, 46.

4. Ibid., 49.

5. Joy Duckett Cain, "Asthma: Fight Back," *Essence,* September 1991, 106.

6. Nancy Hogshead and Gerald S. Couzens, *Asthma and Exercise* (New York: Henry Holt, 1990), 108

7. Bill LeGro, "Take Care of Your Asthma Now," *Prevention,* May 1992, 123.

8. Terrence Monmancy, "Breathe Easier Asthmatics," *Newsweek,* March 21, 1988, 77.

# GLOSSARY

**allergen**—something that triggers an allergic reaction

**allergist**—a medical doctor specializing in the diagnosis and treatment of allergies

**anaphylaxis**—a dangerous, sometimes fatal response to a particular allergen

**antibodies**—proteins in the blood that fight infection and disease

**antihistamine**—a medication used to control allergies

**asthma**—a chronic lung disease largely characterized by difficulty in breathing

**bronchi**—the tubes that carry air into and out of the lungs

**cytotoxic testing**—an unproven diagnostic test for allergies in which a possible allergen is added to a blood sample

**dander**—microscopic flakes of skin that come off animals having fur or feathers

**hay fever**—an allergy to the pollen of some plants, including trees and grass

**histamine**—a biochemical produced by the body that causes sneezing, itchy, watery eyes, and other symptoms

**immune system**—the body's defense mechanism through which harmful substances are battled

**mold**—a type of fungus that triggers an allergic reaction in some people

**perennial allergic rhinitis**—an allergic reaction that continues throughout the year

**seasonal allergic rhinitis**—an allergic reaction that occurs during the warmer weather or pollen season

**sinusitis**—inflammation of the lining of the sinuses

**sulfa drug**—a medication used to fight bacterial infections

# FURTHER
## READING

Dunford, Randall Earl. *Healthy House-Cleaning Tips: Useful Solution to a More Dust-Free Home.* Dallas: NuDawn Publishing, 1992.

Edelson, Edwin. *Allergies.* New York: Chelsea House, 1989

Haas, Francois. *The Essential Asthma Book.* New York: Scribners, 1987.

Krohn, Jacqueline, M.D. *The Whole Way to Allergy Relief Prevention: A Doctor's Complete Guide to Treatment and Self-Care.* Point Roberts, Washington: Hartley & Marks, Inc., 1991.

Newman, Gerald, and Eleanor Layfield. *Allergies.* New York: Franklin Watts, 1992.

Silverstein, Alvin. *Allergies.* New York: Harper and Row, 1977.

# ORGANIZATONS CONCERNED WITH ALLERGIES AND ASTHMA

**Allergy and Asthma Network**
3554 Chain Bridge Road, Ste. 200
Fairfax, VA 22030

**American Academy of Allergy and Immunology**
611 East Wells Street
Milwaukee, WI 53202

**American Association of Immunologists**
9650 Rockville Pike
Bethesda, MD 20814

**American College of Allergists**
800 E. Northwest Hwy., Ste. 101
Mt. Prospect, IL 60056

**American Lung Association**
National Headquarters
1740 Broadway
New York, NY 10019

**Asthma and Allergy Foundation of America**
1125 15th Street, NW, Ste. 502
Washington, DC 20005

**Environmental Protection Agency**
Public Information Service
401 M Street SW
Washington, DC 20460

**National Institute of Allergy and Infectious Diseases**
9000 Rockville Pike
Building 31, Room 7A32
Bethesda, MD 20814

**National Jewish Center for Immunology
and Respiratory Medicine**
1400 Jackson Street
Denver, CO 80206

# I N D E X